Teacher's Resource Book

4

Scott Foresman

Accelerating English Language Learning

Authors

Anna Uhl Chamot

Jim Cummins

Carolyn Kessler

J. Michael O'Malley

Lily Wong Fillmore

Consultant

George González

Longman

ISBN 0-13-028496-3

Pearson Education
10 Bank Street, White Plains, NY 10606

12345678910—CRS—05 04 03 02 01 00

Contents

Oral Language Scoring Rubric

To assess a student's progress, complete a copy of the scale on page 3
at the end of each unit.

	Speaking	Fluency	Structure	Vocabulary	Listening
1	Begins to name concrete objects.	Repeats words and phrases.		Uses isolated words.	Understands little or no English.
2	Expresses personal and survival needs; begins to communicate appropriately in discussions and conversations; begins to recall and retell after listening; asks and responds to simple questions.	Expresses ideas in short phrases; speaks hesitantly because of rephrasing and searching for words.	Uses many sentence fragments; has little control over tenses or other grammatical features.	Uses limited, functional vocabulary.	Understands words and phrases; listens attentively for brief periods; requires much repetition; can follow simple (1 or 2 step) oral directions.
3	Initiates and sustains conversation with descriptors and details; exhibits self confidence in social situations; begins to communicate in classroom situations; recalls, retells, and begins to question after listening.	Speaks with occasional hesitation; begins to develop audience awareness; begins to speak with clarity.	Expresses ideas in complete sentences; applies rules of grammar but lacks control of irregular forms (e.g., "writed," "feets," "not never," "more better").	Uses adequate vocabulary but with some irregular word usage.	Understands classroom discussions with repetition, rephrasing, and clarification; begins to maintain attention during a variety of activities; can follow 2–4 step oral directions.
4	Consistently contributes to classroom discussions and conversations; expresses and supports ideas; errors do not interfere with meaning.	Speaks with near native fluency. Any hesitations do not interfere with communication; demonstrates audience awareness and speaks with clarity and confidence.	Uses a variety of structures with occasional grammatical errors.	Uses varied vocabulary.	Understands most spoken language including classroom discussions; follows complex oral directions.

Oral Language Scoring Scale

Name _____

Date _____

Speaking	1	2	3	4
Fluency	1	2	3	4
Structure	1	2	3	4
Vocabulary	1	2	3	4
Listening	1	2	3	4

Reading Skills/Strategies Checklist

Name _____

Date _____

Skill/Strategy	1st 6 weeks	2nd 6 weeks	3rd 6 weeks	4th 6 weeks	5th 6 weeks	6th 6 weeks
Emergent Reader						
Tracks left/right, up/down.						
Uses pictures to retell storyline.						
Uses predictable patterns to tell/recall story.						
Can locate words in a text.						
Can recognize a few words.						
Developing Reader						
Reads short, predictable texts.						
Begins using reading strategies.						
Begins to self-correct.						
Has small, stable sight vocabulary.						
Displays awareness of sounds/symbols.						
Reader						
Reads familiar material on own.						
Uses several reading strategies.						
Figures out words and self-corrects.						
Has large stable sight vocabulary.						
Understands conventions of writing.						
Independent Reader						
Reads appropriate material independently.						
Uses multiple strategies flexibly.						
Makes inferences; draws conclusions.						
Monitors and self-corrects for meaning.						
Chooses to read.						

Comments

Process Writing Checklist

Name _____   Date _____

Writing Process	1st 6 weeks	2nd 6 weeks	3rd 6 weeks	4th 6 weeks	5th 6 weeks	6th 6 weeks
1. Prewriting Strategies						
Chooses topic before writing.						
Decides purpose for writing.						
Outlines or makes graphic organizer.						
Locates details about topic.						
2. Writing Strategies						
Organizes work and workplace.						
Sets goal for writing.						
Refers to notes and graphic organizer.						
Adapts techniques as necessary (e.g., writes without stopping to correct mistakes).						
3. Postwriting Strategies						
Rereads and reviews.						
Gets feedback from others.						
Rewrites and revises.						
Edits and proofreads.						
4. Applications and Interests						
Communicates in writing (letters, etc.).						
Seeks guidance in writing.						
Writes in all curriculum areas.						
Discusses his/her writing.						
Shares writing with others.						
Edits writing of others.						
Comments						

Written Language Scoring Rubric

To assess a student's progress, complete a copy of the scale on page 7 at the end of each unit.

	Composing	Style	Sentence Formation	Usage	Mechanics
1	No clear central idea or ideas are not apparent to an observer; may be able to read or explain own writing.	Uses known vocabulary in very simple sentences.	Uses frequent nonstandard word order; writing contains many run-on sentences and sentence fragments.	Shifts from one tense to another; errors in basic conventions.	Rereads to check meaning only; misspells even simple words; makes basic errors in punctuation and capitalization.
2	Shows evidence of central ideas but they are not well focused; can read own writing back to an audience.	Uses basic vocabulary that is not purposefully selected; uses mostly simple declarative sentences.	Uses some non-standsrd word order; writing contains some run-on sentences and sentence fragments.	Makes some errors with inflections, agreement, and word meaning.	Begins to make corrections while writing; makes errors in spelling and punctuation that detract from meaning.
3	Focuses on central ideas but they are not evenly elaborated; includes digres-sions; utilizes some kind of organization plan.	Uses more varied vocabulary and structures; writes in a variety of forms; begins to develop a sense of authorship.	Uses mostly standard word order; writing contains few run-on sentences or sentence frag-ments.	Uses mostly standard inflections, agreement, and word meaning.	Recognizes the need to revise and edit and uses revision strategies and the editing process; makes some errors in mechanics that do not detract from meaning.
4	Develops central ideas clearly within an organized and elaborated text; shows confidence as a writer by taking risks.	Purposefully chooses vocab-ulary and sentence variety; employs a distinctive voice to affect reader; initiates independent writing.	Uses standard word order with no run-on sentences or sentence fragments; uses standard modifiers and coordinators and effective transitions.	Uses standard inflections, subject/verb agreement, and standard word meaning.	Uses such conventions as capitalization, punctuation, spelling, and formatting effectively.

Written Language Scoring Scale

Name _____

Date _____

Composing	1	2	3	4
Style	1	2	3	4
Sentence Formation	1	2	3	4
Usage	1	2	3	4
Mechanics	1	2	3	4

Self-Assessment of Oral Language

Name _____

Date _____

Read each statement. Check (✔) the box that is most true for you.

When I use English...	Always	Often	Some-times	Never
Listening				
I can understand many words I hear.				
I can understand the teacher's directions.				
I can understand others when we work in a group.				
I can understand friends outside of class.				
I can understand when the teacher explains something.				
Speaking				
I can name pictures and objects.				
I can ask questions in class.				
I can talk to friends outside of class.				
I can retell a story.				
I can make a presentation in class.				

Self-Assessment of Reading Activities

Name _____

Date _____

Read each statement. Check (✔) the box that is most true for you.

Statement	At Least Once Each Week	At Least Once Each Month	Never or Hardly Ever
I tell a friend about a good book.			
I read about something because I am interested.			
I read on my own outside of school.			
I write about books I have read.			

Statement	Very True of Me	Kind of True of Me	Not at All True of Me
Being able to read is important to me.			
I can understand what I read in school.			
I learn important things from school.			
I am a good reader.			

Other comments about your reading:

_____

_____

_____

Self-Assessment of Writing Activities

Name _____

Date _____

Read each statement. Check (✔) the box that is most true for you.

Statement	At Least Once Each Week	At Least Once Each Month	Never or Hardly Ever
I write letters at home to friends or relatives.			
I take notes when the teacher talks at school.			
I take notes when I read.			
I write a personal response to reading.			
I write a summary of what I read.			
I write stories or poems.			

Statement	Very True of Me	Kind of True of Me	Not at All True of Me
Being able to write is important to me.			
Writing helps me think more clearly.			
Writing helps me tell others what I have learned.			
I am a good writer.			

Other comments about your writing:

_____

_____

_____

My Reading Log

Date	What is the title?	Who is the author?	What did you think of it?

My Writing Log

Date	Working Title	I especially liked:	My readers liked:	What's next?

Anecdotal Record of Reading Skills and Strategies

Name _____

Date _____

Reading Selection

Title _____ Pages _____

Type (circle as many as apply)

fiction	nonfiction	poetry
biography	content text	other:

Context (circle one)

| individual | small group | large group |

Fluency in reading aloud (pauses, miscues, etc.)

Comprehension (recalls main ideas and details)

Strategies (e.g.: uses prior knowledge, predicts, infers meaning, etc.)

Personal response (relates to personal experience)

Recommendations for instruction

Portfolio Conference Questions on Reading

Name _____

Date _____

Reading Selection

Title _____

Type (circle as many as apply)

fiction	nonfiction	poetry
biography	content text	other:

What did you like best in the reading?

What strategies helped you read it?

What do you do to help you remember what you read?

What will you do to become a better reader?

Portfolio Conference Questions on Writing

Name_____

Date_____

Title of writing sample

_____

What do you like best about this piece of writing?

What strategies helped you write it?

How did you choose a topic for writing?

What will you do to become a better writer?

Portfolio Peer Assessment

Name _____

Your partner's name _____

Title of writing sample _____

   1. Read your partner's writing sample.
   2. What do you like best about your partner's writing?

   3. What did your partner do well?

   4. What do you think your partner could make better?

   5. What advice would you give your partner?

Portfolio Self Assessment

Name _____ Date _____

Title of writing sample _____

1. Look at your writing sample.

2. What do you like best about your writing?

3. What did you do well?

4. How could you make your sample better?

5. What are your writing goals? Write one thing you need to do better.

About My Portfolio

1. What I Chose

2. Why I Chose It

3. What I Like and Don't Like

4. How My Work Has Changed

Introduction to the Graphic Organizers

1. **Idea Web:** This can be used for brainstorming activities in which students name the words they know about a topic. It can also be used to organize ideas into groups if circles with subtopics are added around the central circle.

2. **K-W-L Chart:** This can be used to introduce a theme, a lesson, or a reading. It can help generate students' interest in a topic and help students use their prior knowledge as they read. Students can complete the chart at the end of a unit or lesson.

3. **T-Chart:** This chart can be used to help students see relationships between information. It can be used to list cause (left column) and effect (right column) or to list words (right column) associated with a topic or story character (left column).

4. **Venn Diagram:** This can be used to help students understand comparisons and contrasts in a text. It can be used when the question asks, "How are the two things alike? How are they different?"

5. **Story Sequence Chart:** In this chart, students can list the beginning, middle, and end of a story and gain a sense of story structure.

6. **Story Elements Chart:** In this chart, students list the main elements of stories, including setting, characters, problems, and important events.

7. **Main Idea Chart:** This chart can be used to help students see and chart main ideas and supporting details.

8. **Character Trait Web:** In this chart, students can list the important qualities of characters in stories and how the characters' actions reveal those qualities.

9. **Step Chart:** This chart can be used to list events in sequence, such as events in a story or steps in a process.

10. **Problem-Solution Chart:** This chart is used to list problems and solutions in a story.

11. **Word Log:** Students can use this log to list important words in what they are reading or to list words that they want to learn.

Idea Web

K-W-L Chart

Topic:

What We **K**now	What We **W**ant to Know	What We **L**earned

T-Chart

Venn Diagram

_____   _____
- - - - - - - - - - - - - - - -   - - - - - - - - - - - - - - - -
_____   _____

Story Sequence Chart

Beginning

Middle

End

24

Story Elements Chart

Title:

Setting:

Characters:

Problem:

Events:

Solution:

Main Idea Chart

Main Idea

Details

Character Trait Web

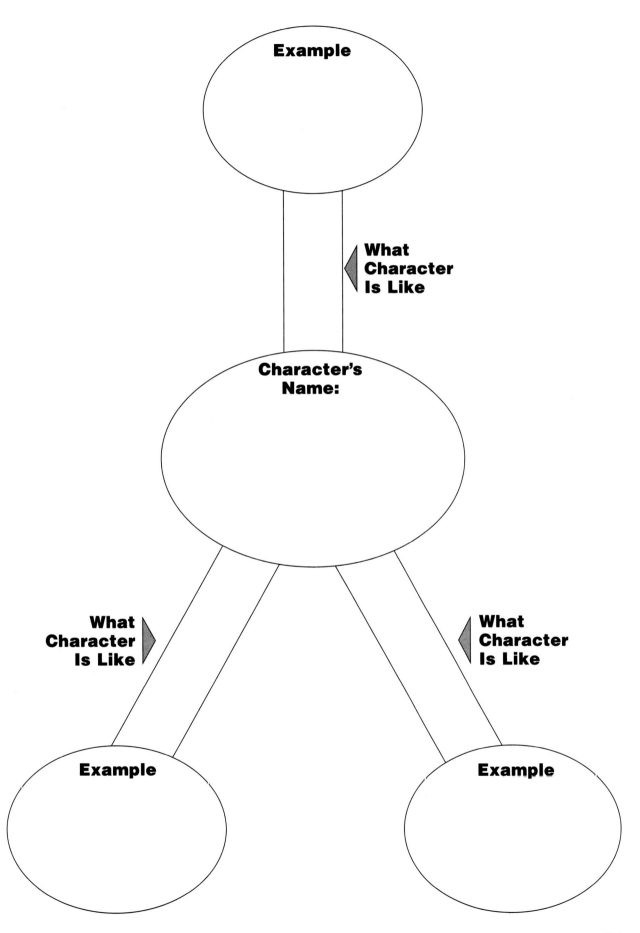

Example

What
Character
Is Like

Character's
Name:

What
Character
Is Like

What
Character
Is Like

Example

Example

Step Chart

_____

- -

How to _____

1.

2.

3.

4.

5.

Problem-Solution Chart

Problem 1:

Solution

Problem 2:

Solution

Problem 3:

Solution

Word Log

Date	New Words I Learned

Chapter Self Assessment

Name _____

Date _____

Chapter number _____

This chapter was about _____

Read each statement. Check (✔) the box that is most true for you.

Statement	Not very well	OK	Well	Very well
I understand the main ideas in the chapter.				
I can ask and answer questions about the main ideas.				
I can tell someone about the main ideas.				
I can write about the main ideas.				

Write something you learned in the chapter.

_____

_____

_____

_____

_____

_____

Dear Family,

Please come to our class on _____ at _____ o'clock

to see _____.

As you know, we have been preparing for this event for several weeks.

Thank you for your interest in our unit project.

Sincerely,

Teacher

You're Invited!

Come to our class on _____

at _____ o'clock.

We will _____

We know you will enjoy seeing our unit project.

Sincerely,

Teacher

Dear Family,

Your child is going to be studying about the West for the next few weeks in school. He or she is going to study about life in the West today as well as the early settlement of the West.

You can work with your child to help him or her learn. You can:

- ask your child what he or she is learning about the West
- read news articles about the West with your child
- watch TV programs that are set in the West and discuss the setting with your child
- take your child on a trip to the supermarket and help him or her identify different foods that are grown in the West

As part of our unit of study, we are going to plan two imaginary trips to the West, one that takes place during the 1800s and one that takes place today.

You can help your child with this project by:

- taking your child to a travel agency or library to obtain information about the West
- providing materials such as craft sticks and scraps of cloth material

Thank you for helping with our study of the West.

Sincerely,

Teacher

Apreciada familia:

Nuestro tema de estudio durante las próximas semanas será el Oeste de los Estados Unidos. Su niño/a estudiará la vida en el Oeste hoy y la vida de los primeros colonos de la región.

Para ayudar a su niño/a en el aprendizaje de este tema, les sugerimos lo siguiente:

- Pregúntenle qué está aprendiendo sobre el Oeste.
- Lean con su niño/a artículos sobre el Oeste.
- Vean juntos programas de televisión que se desarrollan en el Oeste y conversen sobre el lugar.
- Lleven a su niño/a al supermercado y ayúdenle a identificar alimentos que se cultivan en el Oeste.

Como parte de esta unidad, vamos a organizar dos viajes imaginarios al Oeste: uno durante el siglo pasado y otro en la actualidad.

Para colaborar en este proyecto, ustedes podrían:

- llevar a su niño/a a una agencia de viajes o biblioteca para buscar información sobre el Oeste
- suministrar materiales, como paletas de manualidades o retazos de tela

Gracias por ayudarnos a estudiar el Oeste.

Atentamente,

Maestro/a

មកដល់គ្រួសាររបស់សិស្ស

ក្នុងរយៈពេលពីរបីសប្ដាហ៍ខាងមុខនេះ នៅក្នុងសាលា កូនរបស់លោកអ្នកនឹងសិក្សាអំពី តំបន់ប៉េកខាងលិចនៃប្រទេសអាមេរិក ។ គឺកូនរបស់លោកអ្នក នឹងរៀនអំពីជីវិតនៅប៉េកខាងលិច នាពេលបច្ចុប្បន្ន និងការកកើតដំបូងនៃតំបន់ប៉េកខាងលិចនៃប្រទេសអាមេរិក ។

លោកអ្នកអាចជួយកូនឲ្យរៀន ដោយធ្វើដូចតទៅ :

*   សួរកូនថាតើ តើកំពុងរៀនអំពីអ្វីខ្លះនៃប៉េកខាងលិចនោះ
*   អានអត្ថបទទាំងឡាយដែលនិយាយអំពីប៉េកខាងលិច ឲ្យកូនរបស់លោកអ្នកស្ដាប់
*   នាំកូនមើលកម្មវិធីផ្សាយតាមទូរទស្សន៍ ដែលនិយាយអំពីទិដ្ឋភាពនៃប៉េកខាងលិច ហើយពិភាក្សាជាមួយកូន របស់លោកអ្នកអំពី ទិដ្ឋភាពនៅទីនោះ ។
*   នាំកូនទៅផ្សារផ្សំៗដើម្បីបង្ហាញសម្ភារៈទាំងឡាយ ដែលផលិតនៅតំបន់ប៉េកខាងលិច

ដោយវាជាផ្នែកមួយនៃការសិក្សារបស់យើង យើងនឹងធ្វើដំណើរ ជាយក្តីស្រម័យមួយទៅតំបន់ប៉េកខាងលិច ។ ដំណើរលើកទីមួយគឺ ក្នុងឆ្នាំ ១៥០០ ហើយមួយលើកទៀត គឺក្នុងពេលបច្ចុប្បន្ននេះ ។ លោកអ្នកអាចជួយកូនធ្វើដំណើរ ដោយក្តីស្រម័យនេះដោយ:

*   នាំកូនទៅក្រុមហ៊ុនជួយអ្នកធ្វើដំណើរ ឬទៅបណ្ណាល័យ ដើម្បីយកពត៌មានអំពីតំបន់ប៉េកខាងលិច
*   ផ្ដល់ឲ្យកូននូវរបស់ដូចជា: ឈើ ឬដំបងដែលមានភ្នាក់ក្បាច់ និងចន្ទ្រៈក្រណាត់តូចៗ

យើងសូមអរគុណលោកអ្នក ដែលបានជួយដល់ការសិក្សារបស់យើងអំពី
"តំបន់ប៉េកខាងលិចនៃប្រទេសអាមេរិក" ។

ហត្ថលេខា

គ្រូបង្រៀន

Letter to the Family

親愛的家長：

你小孩在下幾個星期裡要學習和西部有關的問題。他們要學習今日西部的生活及早期西部的生活情形。

你能跟小孩一起作下列的活動來幫助他們對這一單元的瞭解：

・問你小孩他們學了那些有關西部的知識

・跟你小孩到超級市場，幫他們辦認那些食物是在西部出產的。

・在這一研讀項目中，我們要作兩次假想到到西部的旅遊。一次發生在一八〇〇年間，另一次發生在現代。

下列的活動能對這一研讀項目有助：

・帶你小孩到旅行社或圖書館索取興西部有關的資料。

・替孩子準備一些可供大家使用的東西，如工藝用的小木條及舊衣物等。

謝謝你對我們「西部」學習單元的幫助。

忠誠地
老師

Cantonese

Chè Paran,

Pitit ou pral aprann kichòy sou teritwa lwès nan kat jewografi pandan semèn ki pral vini yo. Li pral aprann ki jan lwès la ye jodi a ak ki jan li te ye nan tan lontan lè moun te fèk ap abite l.

Ou kapab ede pitit ou aprann si ou:

- Mande l sa li te aprann sou teritwa lwès la.
- Li atik jounal oswa revi sou teritwa lwès avèk li.
- Gade pwogram nan televizyon ki baze nan teritwa lwès la ak pitit ou.
- Mennen pitit ou nan makèt epi ede l idantifye manje ki pwodui nan teritwa lwès la.

Pou fè pati etid nou an, nou pral planifye de (2) vwayaj imajinè nan teritwa lwès la. Youn nan vwayaj yo ap fèt nan ane dizwi san yo (1800) Lòt vwayaj la ap fèt nan ane de mil (2000) lan.

Ou kapab ede pitit ou ak pwojè sa a si ou:

- Mennen pitit ou vizite ajans vwayaj ouswa bibliyotèk pou li jwenn enfòmasyon sou teritwa lwès la.
- Bay pitit ou materyo tankou ti bwa krèm pou bati yo ak moso retay twal.

Mèsi pou èd ou avèk etid nou sou "Teritwa lwès la".

Avèk tout respè,

Pwofesè

Kính thưa quí vị phụ huynh,

Trong vài tuần tới đây, ở trường, cháu sẽ học về đề tài miền Tây. Cháu sẽ học về cuộc sống ở miền Tây hiện nay và đời sống trong thời kỳ ban đầu của cuộc định cư miền Tây ở Hoa Kỳ.

Quí vị có thể giúp cháu học bài này bằng cách sau đây:

• hỏi xem cháu đã học gì về miền Tây
• cùng đọc với cháu vài mẩu tin tức về miền Tây
• cùng cháu xem vài chương trình truyền hình đóng ở miền Tây và cùng bàn với cháu về các bối cảnh của chương trình
• cùng cháu đi chợ để giúp cháu nhận diện các loại thực phẩm, loại trái cây khác nhau trồng ở miền Tây

Trong khuôn khổ của bài học này, chúng tôi dự định làm hai chuyến đi giả tưởng về miền Tây, một chuyến đi thực hiện vào những năm 1800 và một chuyến đi thực hiện trong thời gian hiện tại.

Quí vị có thể giúp cháu làm bài bằng cách:

• cùng với cháu đến văn phòng du lịch hoặc đến thư viện để thu thập các chi tiết về miền Tây
• cung cấp những vật liệu như vài cái que dùng làm thủ công và vài miếng vải vụn để cháu mang vào lớp

Xin cám ơn quí vị đã giúp đỡ cho bài học về miền Tây này.

Thành thật,

Giáo-viên

Name _____

Chapter 1 Language Assessment

A. Read the clue. Choose the answer from the box and write it on the line.

fish	grapefruit	miner
plains	rancher	

1. This person raises cattle. _____

2. This person takes iron ore out of the ground. _____

3. Many farmers live on this landform. _____

4. This kind of crop is grown in Texas. _____

5. Tuna and salmon are kinds of _____ .

B. Write the plural for each of these words.

1. mountain _____   4. pipeline _____

2. fisherman _____   5. shirt _____

3. farmer _____   6. cowgirl _____

C. Write the correct word on the line.

1. Carmen _____ in California.
   live / lives

2. Many fishermen _____ fish in the ocean.
   catch / catches

3. Some farmers _____ grapes.
   grow / grows

Name _____

Chapter 1 Listening Assessment

Listen carefully. Circle what Joe is wearing. Put an X on what Joe sees.

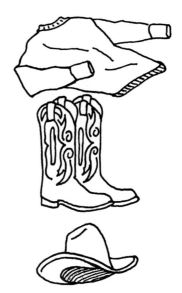

Chapter 2 Language Assessment

A. Read each sentence. Write the correct word on the line.

1. Many people traveled west in _____.

   tents / covered wagons

2. Some _____ moved west to find good farmland.

   settlers / American Indians

3. Many people traveled west on the Oregon _____.

   Trail / Valley

4. People took _____ to fix things.

   soap / tools

5. _____ fires were a terrible problem for settlers.

   Mountain / Prairie

B. Choose words from the box to complete each sentence.
   Write your answer on the line. Use each answer only once.

to find gold	to grow food
to see the horses	to stay warm

1. I am going west. I want _____.
2. My family has a garden. They want _____.
3. We are going to the ranch. We want _____.
4. We put blankets in our wagon. We want _____.

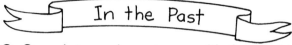
In the Past

C. Complete each sentence with the past tense of the verb in ( ).

1. Yesterday, I _____ my room.

   (clean)

2. Last night, we _____ a cake.

   (bake)

3. Sam _____ to go to the store yesterday.

   (want)

Name _____

Chapter 2 Listening Assessment

Listen carefully. Write the number of the sentence you hear next to the picture it describes.

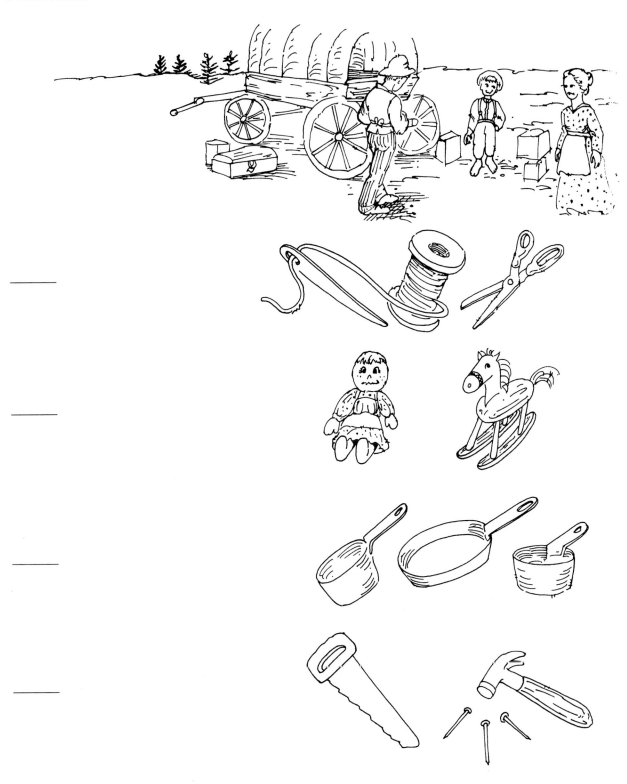

Letter to the Family

Dear Family,

For the next few weeks, your child is going to be studying about living things—cells, plants, animals, and people—and their ecosystems.

You can work with your child to help him or her learn about living things. You can:

- ask your child what he or she is learning about living things
- read news articles about plants and animals with your child
- point out different ecosystems and ask your child to name the different living and nonliving things in them

As part of our study of living things, we are going to present a TV Science Show. We are going to create a poster board display and perform in skits and puppet shows.

You can help your child with this project by:

- helping your child practice for his or her role in a skit or puppet show
- providing old magazines with pictures of living and nonliving things
- providing craft sticks

Thank you for helping with our study of living things.

Sincerely,

Teacher

English

Apreciada familia:

Durante las próximas semanas, su niño/a estudiará en la escuela el tema de los seres vivos: las células, las plantas, los animales y los seres humanos, junto con sus ecosistemas.

Para ayudar a su niño/a en el aprendizaje de este tema, les sugerimos lo siguiente:

- Pregúntenle qué está aprendiendo sobre los seres vivos.
- Lean con su niño/a artículos de noticias sobre animales y plantas.
- Muéstrenle varios ecosistemas y pídanle que nombre sus seres vivos y sus seres no vivos.

Como parte de nuestro estudio de los seres vivos, vamos a organizar un programa de televisión de ciencias. Vamos a hacer una exhibición con cartoncillo, y a representar obras cortas de teatro y de títeres.

Para colaborar en este proyecto, ustedes podrían:

- ayudar a su niño/a a practicar el papel que va a representar
- suministrar revistas viejas con fotografías de seres vivos y seres no vivos
- suministrar paletas de manualidades

Gracias por ayudarnos en el estudio de los seres vivos.

Atentamente,

Maestro/a

មកដល់គ្រួសាររបស់សិស្ស

ក្នុងរយៈពេលពីរបីសប្ដាហ៍ខាងមុខនេះ នៅក្នុងសាលា កូនរបស់លោកអ្នកនឹងសិក្សាអំពី របស់មានជីវិត ដូចជា កោសិកា រុក្ខជាតិ សត្វ មនុស្ស រួមទាំងប្រព័ន្ធនៃជីវិតទាំងនេះ ។

លោកអ្នកអាចជួយកូនឲ្យរៀនអំពីរបស់មានជីវិតនេះ ដោយធ្វើដូចតទៅ :

- សួរកូនថាតើគេកំពុងរៀនអ្វីខ្លះអំពីរបស់មានជីវិត
- អានអត្ថបទ ឬសៀវភៅដែលនិយាយអំពី សត្វនិងរុក្ខជាតិឲ្យកូនស្ដាប់
- បង្ហាញកូនអំពីប្រព័ន្ធខុសៗគ្នានៃជីវិត ហើយសួរកូនឲ្យប្រាប់ឈ្មោះរបស់ណាដែលមានជីវិត និងរបស់ណាដែលគ្មាន ជីវិតនៅក្នុងប្រព័ន្ធទាំងនោះ

ដោយរាជាផ្នែកមួយនៃការសិក្សារបស់យើង យើងនឹងមានកម្មវិធីវិទ្យាសាស្ត្របញ្ចាំងក្នុងទូរទស្សន៍ ។ រួចយើងនឹងបង្កើតរូបភាព ដាក់ តាំង និងសម្ដែងរឿងខ្លីៗ និងរឿងកុក្កុដ្ឋានផងដែរ ។

លោកអ្នកអាចជួយកូនរបស់លោកអ្នកក្នុងកិច្ចការនេះ ដោយធ្វើដូចតទៅ :

- ជួយកូនឲ្យខ្ងិហាត់ ដើរភ្គូដែលគេត្រូវដើរក្នុងការសម្ដែងរឿងទាំងនេះ
- ផ្ដល់ឲ្យកូនទូរសៀវភៅទស្សនារដ្ឋចាស់ៗ ដែលមានរូបភាពៃនរបស់មានជីវិត និងគ្មានជីវិត
- ផ្ដល់សម្ភារៈសំរាប់ដើរភ្គូ ក្នុងការសម្ដែងរឿងដ៏ខ្លីៗនេះ

យើងសូមអរគុណលោកអ្នក ដែលបានជួយដល់ការសិក្សារបស់យើងអំពី "របស់មានជីវិត" ៕

ហត្ថលេខា

គ្រូបង្រៀន

親愛的家長：

在下幾個星期裡，你小孩要學習有關生物的問題—例如有關細胞、植物、動物及人類等—以及生物的生態系統。

爲增加你小孩對生物的認識，你可以在家做下列的活動：

・問你小孩學了那些和生物有關的知識。

・跟小孩一起閱讀有關植物和動物的親聞報導。

・跟小孩指出各種不同的生態系統，問你小孩在那些生態系統中各種生物及無生物的名稱。

在這一研讀項目中，我們計劃作一個科學電視表演節目。我們還要作一份海報展覽，及各種短劇及布袋木偶戲。

你可幫小孩爲這一研讀項目作以下的準備：

・幫你小孩準備他們在短劇或布袋木偶戲中扮演的角色。

・給他看在雜誌中的生物及無生物圖片。

・提供他們一些工藝用的小木條。

謝謝你對我們學習「生物」這一單元的幫助。

忠誠地
　老師

Chè Paran,

Pou semèn k ap vini yo, pitit ou pral aprann sou lavi tankou nan selil, plant, bèt, ak moun, epitou, nan anviwònman y ap viv la.

Ou kapab ede pitit ou aprann sou lavi si ou:

- Mande l ki sa li ap aprann de lavi nan lekòl la.
- Li atik nan jounal oswa revi sou plant avèk bèt ak pitit ou.
- Montre pitit ou diferan vi nan anviwònman an epi mande l pou l idantifye sa k gen vi ak sa k san vi.

Pou fè pati etid nou, nou pral prezante yon pwogram syans nan televizyon. Nou pral fè yon enstalasyon sou yon gwo katon epi yon ti pyès ak yon prezantasyon panten.

Ou kapab ede pitit ou ak pwojè sa a si ou:

- Ede pitit ou pratike pati pa li nan ti pyès panten an.
- Bay pitit ou ansyen revi ak foto bagay ki gen vi ak sa k san vi.
- Ba l ti bwa krèm pou bati.

Mèsi pou èd ou ak etid nou sou "lavi".

Avèk tout respè,

Pwofesè

Kính thưa quí vị phụ huynh,

Trong vài tuần tới đây, ở trường, cháu sẽ học về đề tài những sinh vật, như cây cỏ, thú vật, và con người - và đồng thời cũng học về hệ thống môi sinh của những sinh vật.

Quí vị có thể giúp cháu học về những sinh vật bằng cách sau:

• hỏi xem cháu đang học gì về những sinh vật
• cùng đọc với cháu những mẩu tin tức về những cây cỏ và những thú vật
• nêu ra những hệ thống môi sinh khác nhau và bảo cháu kể tên những sinh vật và những vật không có đời sinh sống trong những hệ thống ấy

Trong khuôn khổ của bài học về những sinh vật, chúng tôi sẽ trình bày một cuộc Trình diễn Khoa học trên truyền hình. Chúng tôi sẽ trưng bày một bích chương và sẽ có vài màn kịch múa rối.

Quí vị có thể giúp cháu trong dự án này bằng cách:

• giúp cháu tập đóng vai trò của cháu trong buổi múa rối
• cung cấp vài tuần báo cũ có hình ảnh của những sinh vật và những vật không có đời sống
• cung cấp vài cái que dùng làm thủ công

Xin cám ơn quí vị giúp đỡ cho bài học những sinh vật này của chúng tôi.

Thành thật,

Giáo-viên

Name _____

Chapter 3 Language Assessment

A. Match the word with its meaning. Write the letter on the line.

1. _____ cells
2. _____ microscope
3. _____ splits
4. _____ energy
5. _____ fungus
6. _____ communicate

a. a plant that doesn't make its own food
b. tiny parts that make up living things
c. what living things need to grow
d. a tool that makes things look bigger
e. use words and sounds
f. divides in two

B. Write the best answer on the line.

1. Right now I _____ a book.
   am reading/read

2. I always _____ lunch at 12 o'clock.
   am eating/eat

3. The bird _____ in the tree right now.
   sings/is singing

4. The bat _____ a lot of mosquitoes every day.
   is catching/catches

5. People _____ words every day.
   are using/use

6. The students _____ bread now.
   are making/make

Chapter 3 Listening Assessment

Listen carefully. Number the items in the order in which Juan saw them.

_____

_____

_____

_____

_____

_____

Chapter 4 Language Assessment

 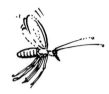 

A. Complete each question with *How much* or *How many.*

1. _____ insects does a bat eat in one day?

2. _____ milk do you drink every day?

3. _____ birds do you see in the tree?

4. _____ food does a cat eat?

B. Choose a word from the box to complete each sentence.
   Write your answer on the line. Use each answer only once.

earthworms	ecosystem
living things	tunnels

1. Plants and animals are _____ .

2. A living thing depends on things in its _____ .

3. _____ live in the ground and eat dead plants.

4. Earthworms dig long _____ .

C. Look at the picture. Use a word from the box to complete each sentence.

in the center of	near	on

1. The chair is _____ the table.

2. A book is _____ the chair.

3. Some flowers are _____ the table.

Chapter 4 Listening Assessment

Listen carefully. Write what you hear.

_____

_____

_____

_____

_____

_____

_____

Dear Family:

For the next few weeks, your child will be learning how early American Indians lived in what is now the United States and Canada. They will also learn about the culture of the Aztec Indians of Mexico.

You can help your child learn by:

- asking your child about what he or she is learning in school
- taking your child to the library and helping him or her find easy-to-read books about American Indians and the Aztecs

As part of their unit of study, the students will be making North American Indian pottery.

You can help your child with this project by talking about pottery and other kinds of crafts that are popular in your homeland. You can also give your child the following items to bring to school:

- plastic forks and knives
- an old shirt or apron your child can wear when he or she makes the pottery

Thank you for your help with our "Early People in North America" unit.

Sincerely,

Teacher

Apreciada familia:

Durante las próximas semanas, su niño/a estudiará en la escuela el tema de los primeros habitantes de Norteamérica: lo que hoy es Estados Unidos, Canadá y parte de México.

Para ayudar a su niño/a en el aprendizaje de este tema, les sugerimos lo siguiente:

- Pregúntenle qué está aprendiendo en la escuela.
- Vayan con su niño/a a la biblioteca y ayúdenle a buscar libros fáciles de leer sobre los indígenas del continente, incluidos los aztecas.

Como parte de esta unidad, los estudiantes harán cerámica indígena.

Para colaborar en este proyecto, ustedes podrían hablar con su niño/a sobre la cerámica y otras artes tradicionales de su país de origen. También podrían darle los siguientes materiales para que traiga a la escuela:

- tenedores y cuchillos de plástico
- una camisa vieja o un delantal que se ponga para trabajar con cerámica

Gracias por ayudarnos en el estudio de la unidad *Early People of North America* ("Los primeros habitantes de Norteamérica").

Atentamente,

Maestro/a

Letter to the Family

មកដល់គ្រួសាររបស់សិស្ស

ក្នុងរយៈពេលពីរបីសប្តាហ៍ខាងមុខនេះ នៅក្នុងសាលា កូនរបស់លោកអ្នកនឹងសិក្សាអំពីរបៀបរស់នៅរបស់ជនជាតិអាមេរិកាំងស្បែក ក្រហម (American Indian) នៅក្នុងសហរដ្ឋអាមេរិក និងកាលណាដាកាលពីជំនាន់ដើម និងនៅពេលបច្ចុប្បន្ន ហើយគេនឹងរៀនអំពីវប្បធម៌របស់ជនជាតិអាមេរិកកាំងស្បែកក្រហម និងជនជាតិម៉ិកស៊ិកូផងដែរ ។

លោកអ្នកអាចជួយឲ្យកូនរៀន ដោយធ្វើដូចតទៅ :

- សួរកូនរបស់លោកអ្នក ថាតើគេកំពុងរៀនអ្វីខ្លះនៅសាលា
- នាំកូនទៅបណ្ណាល័យ ខ្ចីសៀវភៅណាដែលងាយអាន អំពីជនជាតិដើមនៃសហរដ្ឋអាមេរិក និងជនជាតិ Aztecs

ដោយវាជាផ្នែកមួយនៃការសិក្សាអំពីមេរៀននេះ សិស្សទាំងឡាយនឹងធ្វើគ្រឿងក្អមឬឆ្នាំងដីតាមរបៀបជនជាតិអាមេរិកស្បែកក្រហម ។

លោកអ្នកអាចជួយកូនក្នុងកិច្ចការនេះ ដោយនិយាយប្រាប់កូនអំពី ក្អមឬឆ្នាំង រួមទាំងរបស់ធ្វើដោយដៃទាំងឡាយទៀត ដែលសំបូណ៌នៅ ក្នុងមាតុភូមិរបស់លោកអ្នក ។

លោកអ្នកអាចផ្តល់ ឲ្យកូនយកមកសាលានូវរបស់ដូចតទៅ

- សមនិងកាំបិតការ
- ខោអាវ ឬសំពត់ចាស់ៗ សំរាប់ស្លៀកនៅពេលធ្វើឆ្នាំដី

យើងសូមអរគុណលោកអ្នក ដែលបានជួយដល់ការសិក្សារបស់យើងអំពី "មនុស្សជំនាន់ដើមនៃប្រទេសអាមេរិកខាងជើង" ៕

ហត្ថលេខា

គ្រូបង្រៀន

親愛的家長：

你小孩在下幾個星期中要學習一些早期住在現今美國及加拿大的印地安人生活。他們也會學習墨西哥阿茲特克印地安人的文化。

下列的活動能增進你小孩對這一學習單元的了解：

‧問你小孩在學校學了那些和這題目有關的知識。

‧帶你小孩到圖書館找些有關印地安人及阿茲特克人的簡易讀物。

我們會用製造北美印地安人陶瓷器皿作為這一研讀項目作業之一。你若能跟你小孩談論你家鄉常用的陶瓷器皿及其他工藝品，這能幫助他們對這一單元的認識。請將下列物件交給你小孩帶來學校：

‧塑膠刀義

‧舊襯衫或工作圍裙以使他們製造陶瓷器皿時穿用。

謝謝你對我們「北美早期居民」這一單元的幫忙。

忠誠地
老師

Chè Paran,

Pou semèn k ap vini yo, pitit ou pral aprann kichòy sou Premye Endyen Ameriken yo ki t ap viv nan zòn nou rele Etazini ak Kanada kounye a. Epitou, yo pral aprann tou sou kilti endyen Aztèk yo ki te nan zòn Mèksik la.

Ou kapab ede pitit ou aprann si ou:

- Mande pitit ou ki sa l ap aprann lekòl.
- Mennen pitit ou vizite bibliyotèk epi ede li jwenn liv ki fasil pou l li sou Endyen Ameriken yo ak Aztèk yo.

Pou fè pati etid nou, elèv yo pral fè potri (vèsel ki fèt ak tè) tankou endyen nan Amerik Dinò te konn fè.

Ou kapab ede pitit ou ak pwojè sa a si ou pale avèk li sou sa ou konnen sou potri ansanm ak lòt atizay, yo fè nan peyi ou. Ou kapab bay pitit ou sa ki sou lis anba a pou l pote lekòl:

- Fouchèt ak kouto plastik.
- Yon mayo ou pa bezwen osnon yon tabliye pou l mete sou li lè l ap travay ak potri a.

Mèsi pou èd ou ak etid nou sou "Premye pèp nan Amerik Dinò".

Avèk tout respè,

Pwofesè

Kính thưa quí vị phụ huynh,

Trong vài tuần tới đây, cháu sẽ học về đề tài cách sinh sống của những người Mỹ Da Đỏ đầu tiên trên mảnh đất mà ngày nay mình gọi là Hoa Kỳ và Gia Nã Đại. Các học sinh cũng sẽ học về nền văn hóa của thổ dân Aztec của Mễ Tây Cơ.

Quí vị có thể giúp cháu học bài này bằng cách:

- hỏi xem cháu đang học gì ở trường
- cùng với cháu đến thư viện để giúp cháu tìm những quyển sách đọc-dễ-hiểu viết về những người Mỹ Da Đỏ và người Aztec

Trong khuôn khổ của bài học này, các học sinh sẽ làm đồ gốm theo cách thức của người Da Đỏ ở Bắc Mỹ đã làm.

Quí vị có thể giúp cháu làm dự án này bằng cách bàn luận với cháu về đồ gốm và những loại thủ công khác thường thấy có ở quê nhà của quí vị. Đồng thời quí vị có thể cho cháu mang đến trường vài món sau đây:

- vài cái muỗng và dao nhựa
- một cái áo choàng cũ để cháu mặc khi làm đồ gốm

Xin cám ơn quí vị giúp đỡ cho bài học "Người Đầu Tiên ở Bắc Mỹ" này.

Thành thật,

Giáo-viên

Chapter 5 Language Assessment

A. Read the clue. Choose the answer from the box and write it on the line.

archaeologist	buffalo	insulator	plains
pottery	resources	tepee	wigwam

1. the animal the Plains Indians used to meet their needs

   _____

2. a Muskogee shelter made of poles and bark

   _____

3. a Sioux shelter made of buffalo skins _____

4. pots, dishes, and cups made of clay _____

5. a flat, grassy area _____

6. what American Indians used to build their shelters

   _____

7. a scientist who studies how people lived in the past

   _____

8. something that keeps out the heat and cold

   _____

B. Read the sentences. Circle the word the pronoun *they* refers to.

1. The Inuit lived in northern Canada. They made houses of snow.

2. The first Americans made many crafts. They also made weapons.

3. Horses made life easier for the Indians. They used horses to move from place to place.

Chapter 5 Listening Assessment

Listen carefully. Circle the picture for the word you hear.

1.

2.

3.

4.

Chapter 6 Language Assessment

A. Circle the correct answer.

1. Areas on or near mountains are (highlands /lowlands).

2. Aztecs made stone (statues / jewelry) of their gods.

3. Aztecs used (pictographs / calendars) to tell stories.

4. Tamales and tortillas are Aztec (shelters / foods).

B. Read the sentence. Write *before, after, then,* or *when* on the line.

1. The day ——————— Monday is Sunday.

2. Camp begins on July 5, the day ——————— July 4th.

3. ——————— the Aztecs needed things, they went to the market.

4. First the Aztecs made beautiful pottery. ——————— they painted pictures of their gods on the pottery.

C. Complete each sentence with the past tense of the verb in ( ).

1. The Aztecs ——————— beautiful pottery.

    (make)

2. The Aztec farmers ——————— many crops.

    (grow)

3. Papayas and cotton ——————— from the lowlands.

    (come)

4. Each month in the Aztec calendar ——————— twenty days.

    (have)

Name _____

Chapter 6 Listening Assessment

Listen carefully. Write the sentences you hear about an Aztec market.
Then number the pictures for the sentences you heard and wrote.

1. _____

   _____

2. _____

   _____

3. _____

   _____

4. _____

   _____

_____

_____

_____

_____

Dear Family,

For the next few weeks, your child is going to be learning about food, nutrition, and the digestive system.

You can work with your child to help him or her learn. You can:

- ask your child what he or she is learning about food
- discuss with your child how eating the right kinds of food in the right amounts is important for good health
- take your child food shopping and help him or her read the ingredient labels on packages

As part of our unit of study, we are going to make a multicultural cookbook. You can help your child complete his or her part in the project by:

- providing a simple recipe from your country of origin
- helping your child understand the recipe so that he or she can write it in English

Thank you for helping us with our "Food" unit.

Sincerely,

Teacher

Apreciada familia:

Durante las próximas semanas, su niño/a estudiará en la escuela el tema de los alimentos, la nutrición y el aparato digestivo.

Para ayudar a su niño/a en el aprendizaje de este tema, les sugerimos lo siguiente:

• Pregúntenle qué está aprendiendo sobre la alimentación.
• Explíquenle que comer buenos alimentos en las cantidades debidas es importante para la buena salud.
• Lleven a su niño/a a la compra y pídanle que lea los ingredientes de los paquetes o léanlos juntos.

Como parte de esta unidad, vamos a hacer un libro de recetas de cocina de muchas partes del mundo. Para ayudar a su niño/a a hacer su parte de este proyecto, ustedes podrían:

• darle una receta sencilla de su país de origen
• ayudarle a entender la receta para que la escriba en inglés

Gracias por ayudarnos en el estudio de la unidad *"Food"* ("Los alimentos").

Atentamente,

Maestro/a

មកដល់គ្រួសាររបស់សិស្ស

ក្នុងរយៈពេលពីរបីសប្ដាហ៍ខាងមុខនេះ នៅក្នុងសាលា កូនរបស់លោកអ្នកនឹងសិក្សាអំពី ចំណីអាហារ ជីវជាតិ និងប្រព័ន្ធរំលាយ អាហាររបស់មនុស្ស ។

លោកអ្នកអាចជួយកូនឲ្យរៀន ដោយធ្វើដូចតទៅ

- សួរកូនថាតើគេកំពុងរៀនអ្វីអំពីចំណីអាហារ
- ពិភាក្សាជាមួយកូនអំពីរបៀបបរិភោគអាហារល្អៗ និងចំនួនឲ្យសមល្មម ដើម្បីឲ្យមានសុខភាពល្អ ព្រោះវាសំខាន់ណាស់សំរាប់ជីវិត
- នាំកូនទៅទិញម្ហូប ហើយជួយបង្រៀនគេឲ្យអានផ្លាក ដែលរៀបរាប់អំពីគ្រឿងទេម្ហូប ដែលបិទជាប់នឹងម្ហូបអាហារ ទាំងឡាយ ។

ដោយវាជាផ្នែកមួយនៃការសិក្សារបស់យើង យើងនឹងបង្កើតសៀវភៅធ្វើម្ហូបអាហារ ចំរុះវប្បធមិមួយ ។ ដូច្នេះ លោកអ្នកអាចជួយ កូនក្នុងកិច្ចការនេះ ដោយ:

- បង្រៀនកូនទទួរបបមន្ត ឬរបៀបធ្វើម្ហូបជីដាយស្រួលមួយ តាមរប្បធមិរបស់លោកអ្នក
- ជួយពន្យល់កូនឲ្យយល់អំពីរបៀបធ្វើម្ហូបនេះ ដើម្បីឲ្យកូនសរសេរជាភាសាអង់គ្លេស

យើងសូមអរគុណលោកអ្នក ដែលបានជួយដល់ការសិក្សារបស់យើងអំពី "ចំណីអាហារ" ។

ហត្ថលេខា

គ្រូបង្រៀន

親愛的家長：

你的小孩在下幾個星期中要學習關於食物、營養及消化系統。
下列的活動能增進你小孩對這單元的了解：

・問你小孩學了那些與食物有關的知識。

・跟小孩討論吃適當與適量食物對身體健康的重要。

・帶孩子去購買食物，教導他們閱讀在食物包裝上書寫的各種材
　料。

我們要用編寫一本多元文化食譜作為這一單元的作業之一，你可幫
你孩子完成下面的功課：

・交給你小孩一份來自你家鄉的簡易食譜。

・跟你小孩說明那份食譜，然後叫他們用英文寫下那份食譜。

謝謝你對我們「食物」這一單元的幫忙。

忠誠地
老師

Chè Paran,

Pou semèn k ap vini yo, pitit ou pral aprann tout sa pou l konnen sou manje, nitrisyon ak sistèm dijesyon.

Ou kapab ede pitit ou aprann si ou:

- Mande l ki sa li te aprann sou manje.
- Diskite ak pitit ou ki jan lè ou manje sa ki bon pou ou, nan kantite rezonab, enpòtan pou sante ou.
- Mennen pitit ou ale fè makèt. Ede l pou l li engredyen yo sou etikèt yo ak bwat yo.

Pou fè pati etid nou, nou pral fè yon liv resèt ak manje tout kalite kilti. Ou kapab ede pitit ou konplete pati pa li nan pwojè sa a si ou:

- Ba li resèt senp ki sòti nan peyi ou.
- Ede pitit ou konprann resèt la byen pou li kapab ekri li ann Anglè.

Mèsi pou èd ou nan etid nou sou "Manje".

Avèt tout respè,

Pwofesè

Kính thưa quí vị phụ huynh,

Trong vài tuần tới đây, cháu sẽ học về đề tài thực phẩm, sự dinh dưỡng, và hệ thống tiêu hóa.

Quí vị có thể giúp cháu học bài này bằng cách:

- hỏi xem cháu đang học gì về thực phẩm
- thảo luận với cháu về tầm quan trọng của việc nên dùng loại thực phẩm nào cho đúng và nên dùng đúng số lượng nào để giữ gìn cho sức khỏe tốt
- dẫn cháu đi mua thực phẩm và giúp cháu đọc bản ghi thành phần các chất có in trên các gói

Trong khuôn khổ của bài học này, chúng tôi sẽ soạn một quyển sách dạy nấu ăn của dân các nước có nền văn hóa khác nhau (đa văn hóa). Quí vị có thể giúp phần của cháu trong dự án này bằng cách:

- cung cấp một công thức nấu một món ăn thuần túy của quê hương gốc của quí vị
- giúp cháu hiểu cái công thức ấy để cháu biên ra bằng tiếng Anh

Xin cám ơn quí vị giúp đỡ cho bài học "Thực Phẩm" này.

Thành thật,

Giáo-viên

Chapter 7 Language Assessment

A. Choose an answer from the box to complete each sentence.
   Use each answer only once.

balanced diet	energy	food pyramid
carbohydrates	fats	proteins

1. People need _____ for walking, running, and playing.

2. To stay healthy, you need to eat a _____.

3. Butter, oils, and sweets have _____.

4. Cereal, bread, rice, and pasta have _____.

5. Meat, fish, and nuts have _____.

6. A _____ can help you choose foods that are good to eat.

B. Answer each question with a short sentence.
   Use the pictures to help you. See the example.

Did María drink her milk?

Yes, she did. _____

1. Did the children eat lunch in the cafeteria?

   _____

2. Did Joe eat an apple?

   _____

3. Did Mrs. Lewis buy some carrots?

   _____

Chapter 7 Listening Assessment

Listen carefully and circle the ten foods that Kim and her mother bought at the grocery store.

Chapter 8 Language Assessment

A. Choose the answer from the box and write it on the line.

| chew | saliva | vitamins |
| digestion | stomach | |

1. Before you swallow a piece of an apple, you _____ it.

2. After you eat, your _____ is full of food.

3. _____ happens when your body breaks down the food you eat.

4. The _____ in your mouth makes food soft so that you can swallow it.

5. _____ are nutrients that help cure diseases.

B. Look at the picture. Then choose a word from the box to complete the sentence. Use each answer only once.

| across | in the distance | next to | on |

1. The school is _____ the street from the toy store.

2. A car is _____ the street.

3. A fruit stand is _____ the school.

4. The bus is _____.

Name _____

Chapter 8 Listening Assessment

Listen carefully. Write what you hear.

_____

_____

_____

_____

_____

_____

_____

_____

Letter to the Family

Dear Family,

Your child is going to be learning about rain forests for the next few weeks in school. He or she is going to study about why rain forests are important and what people are doing to protect them.

You can work with your child to help him or her learn. You can:

- ask your child what he or she is learning about the rain forests
- help your child identify rain forest products found in your home
- take your child to the library to find books about protecting rain forests. One such book is *Fifty Simple Things Kids Can Do to Save the Earth* by John Javna (Andrews and McMeel, 1990).

As part of our study of the rain forests, we are going to plan a "Save the Rain Forests" campaign. You can help by:

- providing your child with a rain forest product you may have at home, such as a tropical fruit or spice
- cutting out pictures of rain forest products from old magazines

Thank you for helping us with our "Rain Forests" unit.

Sincerely,

Teacher

English

Apreciada familia:

Durante las próximas semanas, su niño/a estudiará en la escuela el tema de las selvas tropicales. Vamos a estudiar por qué son importantes y qué se está haciendo para protegerlas.

Para ayudar a su niño/a en el aprendizaje de este tema, les sugerimos lo siguiente:

- Pregúntenle qué está aprendiendo sobre las selvas tropicales.
- Ayúdenle a identificar productos de las selvas tropicales en su casa.
- Vayan juntos a la biblioteca a buscar libros sobre la protección de las selvas tropicales, como por ejemplo: Ecología para niños, de The EarthWorks Group.

Como parte de nuestro estudio de esta unidad, vamos a organizar una campaña titulada "Salvar las selvas tropicales". Para colaborar en este proyecto, ustedes podrían:

- darle a su niño/a un producto de la selva tropical que tengan en casa, como una fruta o una especia tropical
- recortar en revistas viejas fotografías de productos tropicales

Gracias por ayudarnos en el estudio de la unidad "*Rain Forests*" ("Las selvas tropicales").

Atentamente,

Maestro/a

មកដល់គ្រួសាររបស់សិស្ស

ក្នុងរយៈពេលពីរបីសប្តាហ៍ខាងមុខនេះ នៅក្នុងសាលា កូនរបស់លោកអ្នកនឹងសិក្សាអំពី តំបន់ភ្លៀងធ្លាក់និងព្រៃភ្នំ (Rain Forests) គឺគេនឹងរៀនអំពីមូលហេតុ ដែលតំបន់ភ្លៀងធ្លាក់ និងព្រៃភ្នំ មានសារៈសំខាន់ដល់យើង និងអ្វីដែលយើងរាល់គ្នាអាចធ្វើ ដើម្បីរក្សាការពារតំបន់ទាំងនោះ ។

លោកអ្នកអាចជួយកូនឱ្យរៀន ដោយធ្វើដូចតទៅ :

- សួរកូនថាតើ គេកំពុងរៀនអំពីអ្វីខ្លះ ៃនតំបន់ភ្លៀងធ្លាក់ និងព្រៃភ
- ជួយបង្ហាញកូនទូរវត្ថុនៅក្នុងផ្ទះ ដែលបានមកពីតំបន់ទាំងនោះ
- នាំកូនទៅបណ្ណាល័យ ខ្ចីសៀវភៅដែលនិយាយអំពី វិធីរក្សាការពារតំបន់ភ្លៀងធ្លាក់និងព្រៃភ្នំ មកអានជាមួយកូន ។ សៀវភៅមួយដែលនិយាយអំពីរឿងនេះ មានចំណងជើងថា: Fifty Simple Things Kids Can Do to Save the Earth by John Javna (Andrews and McMeel, 1990) វិធីដ៏ងាយស្រួលហាសិបម៉្យាង ដែលក្មេងអាចធ្វើ ដើម្បីការពារ និងរក្សាផែនដីរបស់យើង ដែលនិពន្ធដោយលោក John Javna

ដោយវាជាផ្នែកមួយៃនការសិក្សាអំពីមេរៀននេះ យើងនឹងធ្វើពិធីយាសនាបញ្ចុះបញ្ចូលមួយ ។ លោកអ្នកអាចជួយ ដោយធ្វើដូចត ទៅ :

- ផ្តល់ឱ្យកូនទូរវរបស់ទាំងឡាយ ដែលធ្វើឡើបុបានមកពីតំបន់ភ្លៀងធ្លាក់និងព្រៃភ្នំ ដូចជា: ផ្ទៃលើ បុ្រគ្រឿងសម្ព
- កាត់រូបភាពទាំងឡាយៃនតំបន់ភ្លៀងធ្លាក់និងព្រៃភ្នំ ដែលមាននៅក្នុងទស្សនាវដ្តីចាស់ៗ ឱ្យកូន

យើងសូមអរគុណលោកអ្នក ដែលបានជួយដល់ការសិក្សារបស់យើងអំពី "តំបន់ភ្លៀងធ្លាក់និងព្រៃភ្នំ" ។។

ហត្ថលេខា

គ្រូបង្រៀង

親愛的家長：

你的孩子在下幾個星期內要學習各種房屋，建築材料及工具。

下面的活動能幫你小孩學習這一題目：

- 跟孩子談論你們家是用甚麼材建造的，及用這些建材的原因。
- 跟孩子談論你們家鄉的房屋是用甚麼材料建造的，及爲甚麼要用那些建材。
- 讓孩子們看看你們家常用的工具，以及這些工具使用的方法。

這一單元的作業包括作一項「世界各地的房屋」的展覽。班上的同學會分成不同小組。每組選擇一個國家作展覽對家。這個展覽會包括有關國家的天然資源，氣候及最常見的房屋。

下列是你可以幫你小孩準備這一研讀項目作業的方法：

- 帶你小孩到圖書館尋找他們小組選出那國家的資料。資料應包括該國的自然資源、氣候及房屋的形式。

(圖書館員通常都能幫你找適當資料)。

- 替你小孩收集小樹枝、石塊和其他天然資料，讓小孩將這些東西帶來學校。
- 叫小孩帶下列任何一樣東西來學校：冰棒木條、紙盒紙塊及吸管。

謝謝你對我們「住屋」一單元的幫忙。

忠誠地
老師

Chè Paran,

Pitit ou pral aprann tout sa pou l konnen sou "rain forests" nan semèn k ap vini yo. Pitit ou pral etidye poukisa "rain forests" yo enpòtan epi ki sa moun ap fè pou pwoteje yo.

Ou kapab ede pitit ou aprann si ou:

- Mande pitit ou ki sa li te aprann sou "rain forests" yo.
- Ede pitit ou idantifye pwodui ou genyen lakay ou, ki sòti nan "rain forests".
- Mennen pitit ou nan bibliyotèk pou jwenn liv sou ki jan moun ka pwoteje "rain forests" yo. Yon liv ou ka jwenn se "Senkant bagay senp timoun ka fè pou sove latè a" (Fifty Simple Things Kids Can Do to Save the Earth by John Javna (Andrews and McMeel, 1990).

Pou fè pati etid nou sou "rain forests" yo, nou pral fè plan pou nou fè yon kanpay pou "Sove 'rain forests' yo" Ou kapab ede si ou:

- Bay pitit ou yon pwodui ou ka gen lakay ou, ki sòti "rain forests" nan, tankou fwi twopikal osnon epis.
- Koupe foto pwodui "rain forests" nan revi ou pa bezwen.

Mèsi pou èd ou avèk etid nou sou "rain forests".

Avèk tout respè,

Pwofesè

Kính thưa quí vị phụ huynh,

Trong vài tuần tới đây, ở trường, cháu sẽ học về đề tài các khu rừng mưa. Cháu sẽ học tại sao những khu rừng mưa quan trọng và người ta đang làm gì để bảo vệ những khu rừng này.

Quí vị có thể giúp cháu học bài này bằng cách:

• hỏi xem cháu đang học gì về những khu rừng mưa
• giúp cháu nêu tên những sản phẩm của khu rừng mưa đang có trong nhà
• dẫn cháu đến thư viện để tìm những quyển sách biên về sự bảo vệ khu rừng mưa.
  Có một quyển sách về loại này là *Fifty Simple Things Kids Can Do to Save the Earth* do John Javna biên soạn (Andrews and McMeel, 1990)

Trong khuôn khổ của bài học những khu rừng mưa này, chúng tôi dự định làm một chiến dịch "Giữ Gìn Khu Rừng Mưa". Quí vị có thể giúp bằng cách:

• cung cấp cho cháu một sản phẩm của khu rừng mưa mà quí vị có trong nhà, như một loại trái cây hoặc một món gia vị của vùng nhiệt đới
• cắt vài bức ảnh về rừng mưa trong các tuần báo cũ

Xin cám ơn quí vị giúp đỡ cho bài học "Rừng Mưa" này.

Thành thật,

Giáo-viên

Name _____

Chapter 9 Language Assessment

A. Match the word with its meaning. Write the letter on the line.

1. _____ solar energy

2. _____ food chain

3. _____ rain forests

4. _____ latex

5. _____ species

6. _____ equator

a. warm, rainy areas where many trees, plants, and animals are found

b. kinds of plants and animals

c. movement of energy from the sun to plants to animals

d. imaginary line around the middle of the Earth

e. energy that comes from the sun

f. white, milky juice that comes from the rubber tree

B. Write the best answer on the line.

1. The bug is _____ than the leaf.
   small/smaller

2. Trail C is the _____ of the three trails.
   long/longest

3. In the rain forests, frogs are _____ to see than monkeys.
   hardest/harder

4. Howler monkeys are _____ than other monkeys in the rain forest.
   noisier/noisiest

Name _____

Chapter 9 Listening Assessment

Listen carefully. Draw Antonio's path through the rain forest.

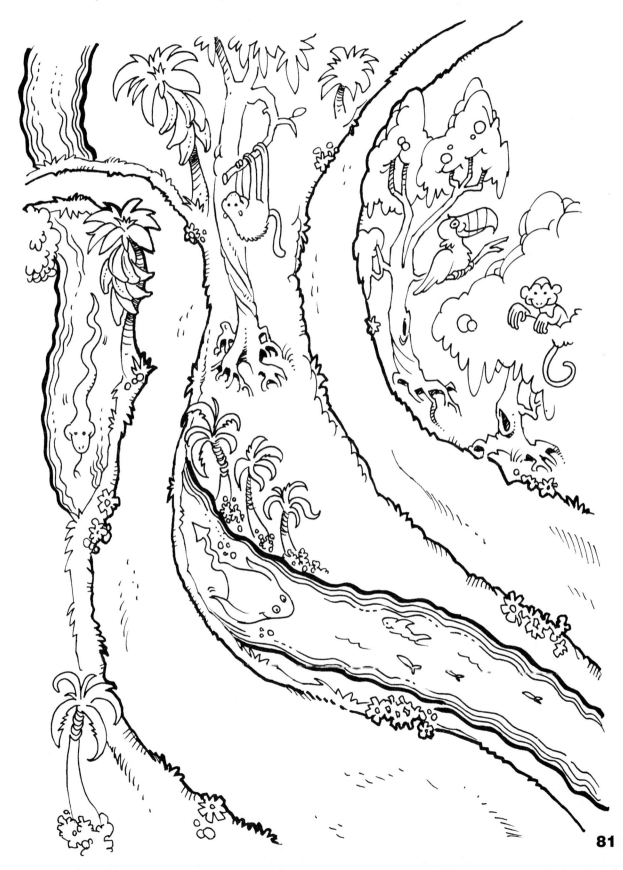

Name _____

Chapter 10 Language Assessment

A. Choose a word from the box to complete the sentence.
   Use each word only once.

crops	lumber	minerals
papayas	rubber	spices

1. People use _____ to make furniture and houses.

2. Farmers clear the land to grow _____.

3. Miners clear the land to dig for copper, gold, and other
   _____.

4. Bananas and _____ are fruits we get from the rain
   forests.

5. Erasers and balls are made of _____.

6. _____ such as cinnamon and nutmeg grow in the
   rain forests.

B. Write the best answer on the line.

1. In the 1960s, people _____ roads into the
   rain forests.   built/is building

2. In the 1960s, lumber companies and ranchers
   _____ many trees.
   cut down/are cutting

3. Now many people _____ to save the rain
   forests.   worked/are working

4. Today, people _____ products from trees.
          harvested/are harvesting

Name _____

Chapter 10 Listening Assessment

Listen carefully. Circle the rain forest products you hear.

coconuts   grapes   bananas   pineapple

lemons   strawberries   mangoes   papayas

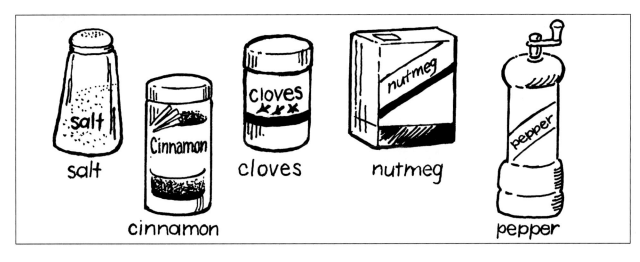

salt   cloves   nutmeg   pepper

cinnamon

vegetable oil   mustard   nuts   coffee beans

cheese

Dear Family,

For the next few weeks, your child will learn about the regions and states of the United States, including your state.

You can help your child by:

- asking him or her to show you on a map the region and the state where you live
- talking about the places you have visited or would like to visit in your state

At the completion of the unit, we plan to have a "State Fair." The "State Fair" will include displays about our state. You can help your child find any of the following items about your state:

- travel brochures or posters
- post cards
- state maps

In addition, we want our students to know about their countries of origin. You can share this kind of information with your child by:

- using a map of your country of origin to point out the capital city and explain the divisions of your country, such as provinces, departments, or states
- talking about the products your country produces
- talking about your country's symbols

Thank you for your help with our "Regions and States" unit.

Sincerely,

Teacher

English

Letter to the Family

Apreciada familia:

Durante las próximas semanas, su niño/a estudiará el tema de las regiones y los estados que conforman los Estados Unidos, incluido nuestro estado.

Para ayudar a su niño/a podrían:

- pedirle que señale en un mapa la región y el estado donde viven
- hablar de los lugares del estado que han visitado o que desearían visitar

Al final de la unidad planeamos realizar una "Feria del estado" con muestras representativas de la región. Para colaborar en este proyecto, pueden ayudar a su niño/a a conseguir alguno de los siguientes objetos acerca de nuestro estado:

- folletos o afiches turísticos
- postales
- mapas del estado

Asimismo, deseamos que nuestros estudiantes sepan acerca de sus países de origen. Para tal fin, les sugerimos:

- mostrarle a su niño/a en un mapa la ciudad capital de su país de origen y explicarle cómo está dividido, ya sea en provincias, departamentos o estados
- hablarle de los productos que su país genera
- hablarle de los símbolos patrios

Gracias por ayudarnos con nuestra unidad *Regions and States* ("Regiones y estados").

Atentamente,

Maestro/a

មកដល់គ្រួសាររបស់សិស្ស

ក្នុងរយៈពេលពីរបីសប្ដាហ៍ខាងមុខនេះ កូនរបស់លោកអ្នកនឹងសិក្សាអំពីតំបន់នានា និងឈ្មោះរដ្ឋទាំងឡាយនៅក្នុងសហរដ្ឋអាមេរិក រួម ទាំងរដ្ឋដែលលោកអ្នកកំពុងរស់នៅនេះផងដែរ ។

លោកអ្នកអាចជួយកូនរបស់ខ្លួនដោយធ្វើដូចតទៅនេះ៖

- សួរកូនឱ្យរាវ៉ាងរកដ្ឋនៅក្នុងផែនទី បង្ហាញដល់លោកអ្នកកូនរវតំបន់ និងរដ្ឋដែលកំពុងរស់នៅ
- និយាយប្រាប់កូនអំពីទីកន្លែងដែលខ្លួនបានទៅលេង ឬក៏មានបំណងទៅលេង ដែលស្ថិតនៅក្នុងរដ្ឋនេះ ។

នៅចុងបញ្ចប់នៃកម្មវិធីនេះ យើងមានគំរោងមួយ គឺរៀបចំ "ការដាក់តាំងទិដ្ឋភាពនៃរដ្ឋទាំងឡាយ" ។ ហើយការដាក់តាំងនេះ នឹងមានរូបបញ្ជាំងទាំងទិដ្ឋភាពនៃរដ្ឋដែលយើងកំពុងរស់នៅនេះផងដែរ ។ ដូច្នេះ លោកអ្នកអាចជួយក្នុងកម្មវិធីនេះ ដោយជួយរក ឱ្យកូន នូវរូបតានាពីរដ្ឋរបស់យើង មានដូចខាងក្រោមនេះ៖

- កូនសៀវរភាពីតមានអំពីការធ្វើដំណើរ ឬរូបភាពនៃការធ្វើដំណើរ
- កាតប៉ុស្តាល់
- ផែនទីនៃរដ្ឋទាំងឡាយ

លើសពីនេះទៀត យើងចង់ឱ្យសិស្សទាំងឡាយបានស្គាល់ប្រទេសកំណើតរបស់គេផងដែរ ។ ដូច្នេះ លោកអ្នកអាចជួយបង្រៀន កូនរបស់ខ្លួនដោយ៖

- ប្រើផែនទីនៃប្រទេសរបស់លោកអ្នក ដើម្បីចង្អុលបង្ហាញទីតាំងនៃរដ្ឋធានី ឬទីឡ្យ់នូវរបៀបបែងចែកនៃប្រទេសរបស់លោក អ្នក ដូចជា ៖ ការបែងចែកចេញជាស្រុក ជាឃុំ ជាខេត្ត ឬជារដ្ឋជាដើម ។
- និយាយពីភាគផលទាំងឡាយ ដែលផលិតនៅក្នុងប្រទេសរបស់លោកអ្នក ។
- ប្រាប់កូនអំពីរូប ឬសញ្ញាសំណាងប្រទេសរបស់លោកអ្នក ។

យើងសូមអរគុណដល់លោកអ្នក ដែលបានជួយក្នុងកម្មវិធីសិក្សាអំពី តំបន់និងភូមិភាគនៃរដ្ឋទាំងឡាយរបស់យើង ៕

ហត្ថលេខា

គ្រូបង្រៀន

親愛的家長：

　　在下幾個星期中，你小孩在學校要學習有關環境問題。這一學習單元包括有絕種危險性的動物，各種環境污染問題，及環境保護問題。

　　下列是可以幫助你小孩增加對環境認識的方法：

・問你小孩他們學了那些與環境有關的知識

・跟你小孩談論環境污染及防止環境污染的方法

・在家裡讓小孩重新利用廢物。

　　在這一學習單元中，我們計劃作一「地球日」的慶祝。我們要展出我們對環境有關的功課。如果你能讓小孩帶一、二樣下列的物件來學校，對我們學習這一單元，會有很大的幫助：

・用過的鉛罐

・空的牛奶盒

・有蓋子的空玻璃瓶

・衣夾

・瓶蓋

・有循環使用記號的紙盒或塑膠盒子

　　我們希望你能跟我們一起慶祝「地球日」、我們希望你能帶一件能循環使用的物件來作為入場門票。

　　你可以帶一個玻璃瓶，一個鋁罐，或一份舊報紙等。

　　謝謝你對「保護地球」這一單元的幫忙。

忠誠地

老師

Chè paran,

Pou semèn k ap vini yo, pitit ou pral aprann rejyon yo ak eta ki nan Etazini ansanm ak eta pa w la tou.

Ou kapab ede pitit ou si w:

- Mande pitit ou pou montre w, sou yon kat, rejyon ak eta kote ou rete.
- Pale ak pitit ou de kote ou te vizite ouswa kote ou ta renmen vizite nan eta ou rete a.

Nan fen pati sa a, nou gen plan pou nou fè yon "State Fair". "State Fair" sa a ap genyen ladan enstalasyon sou chak eta yo. Ou kapab ede pitit ou jwenn youn nan bagay ki nan lis anba a sou eta kote ou rete a:

- Liv enfòmasyon sou vwayaj ouswa gwo foto ki montre kote ou ka vizite nan eta a.
- Kat postal ki montre foto kote ou ka jwenn nan eta ou rete a.
- Kat eta a.

Anplis, nou vle elèv yo konnen rejyon ki nan peyi yo. Ou kapab pataje enfòmasyon sa yo ak pitit ou:

- Gade yon kat peyi kote ou moun. Montre pitit ou kote kapital vil la ye sou kat la epi esplike divizyon peyi a tankou, pwovens, depatman, ouswa eta yo.
- Pale de kalite pwodui peyi ou fè.
- Pale de senbòl ki nan peyi ou.

Mèsi pou èd ou avèk etid nou sou "Rejyon ak Eta".

Avèk tout respè,

Pwofesè

Kính thưa quí vị phụ huynh,

Trong vài tuần lễ tới đây, con em quí vị sẽ học về các vùng và các tiểu bang của Hoa Kỳ, kể cả cái tiểu bang mà quí vị đang ở.

Quí vị có thể giúp cháu học bằng cách:

• bảo cháu chỉ trên bản đồ cái vùng và cái tiểu bang mà quí vị đang ở.
• nói đến những nơi quí vị đã viếng qua hoặc dự định sẽ viếng đến trong tiểu bang của quí vị.

Vào cuối đơn vị học này chúng tôi dự tính sẽ có một "Hội Chợ Tiểu Bang". Cái hội chợ này sẽ bao gồm các gian hàng chưng bày về tiểu bang của chúng ta. Quí vị có thể giúp cháu tìm những món sau đây về tiểu bang của quí vị:

• các báo quảng cáo hoặc các bích chương du lịch
• hình cảnh gởi qua bưu điện
• bản đồ của tiểu bang

Thêm nữa, chúng tôi muốn các em học sinh biết về quê hương xứ sở của các em. Quí vị có thể chia sẻ loại hiểu biết này cho cháu bằng cách:

• dùng bản đồ của quê hương xứ sở của quí vị để chỉ thủ đô và cách phân chia đất nước ra thành tỉnh, miền, làng, quận ra sao
• kể ra tên các sản phẩm địa phương của xứ sở quí vị
• nói về cái biểu chương của xứ sở quí vị

Xin cám ơn quí vị đã giúp đỡ cho bài học "Các Vùng và Các Tiểu bang" này.

Thành thật,

Giáo viên

Chapter 11 Language Assessment

A. Read each sentence. Write the correct word on the line.

1. The arrow is pointing _____.

   north/south

2. The arrow is pointing _____.

   east/west

3. The Northeast is a _____.

   region/state

4. People catch fish on the _____.

   mountain/coast

5. A flag and a bird are state _____.

   names/symbols

6. The city where state laws are made is the state

   _____.

   capital/park

B. Look at the picture. Choose a word from the box.
   Write the correct word on the line

a lot of	each	some

1. _____ person in my family has a map.

2. _____ of the crops in the South are peanuts and oranges.

3. There are _____ animals at the zoo.

Chapter 11 Listening Assessment

Listen carefully. Write what you hear.

_____

_____

_____

_____

_____

_____

_____

_____

Name _____

Chapter 12 Language Assessment

A. Read each question. Circle the answer or answers in each box.

1. Which words tell about the past?

| long ago | history | last year | tomorrow |

2. Which words tell about the present?

| today | right now | in the past |

3. What do you call a person who comes to a place for the first time?

| explorer | "forty-niner" | trapper | American |

4. What shows events and their dates in history?

| map key | time line | symbols |

5. How can you learn about the past?

| visit places | read books | talk to people |

B. Complete each sentence with the past tense of the verb in ( ).

1. Many settlers _____ to California.
   (come)

2. Some people _____ houses from logs.
   (build)

3. Some people _____ wagon trains to California.
   (drive)

4. Many people _____ happy to find gold in 1849.
   (are)

Name _____

Chapter 12 Listening Assessment

Listen carefully. Circle the correct date for each event you hear.

1. Mexico claimed California.   1812   1822   1824

2. Gold was found.   1840   1845   1848

3. California became a state.   1850   1855   1860

4. Disneyland opened.   1948   1952   1955

5. The Olympic Games were in   1981   1984   1990
   Los Angeles.

6. An earthquake hit Los Angeles.   1989   1994   1995

Test Answers

Language Assessment

page 40:
- A. 1. rancher
     2. miner
     3. plains
     4. grapefruit
     5. fish
- B. 1. mountains
     2. fishermen
     3. farmers
     4. pipelines
     5. shirts
     6. cowgirls
- C. 1. lives
     2. catch
     3. grow

page 42:
- A. 1. covered wagons
     2. settlers
     3. Trail
     4. tools
     5. Prairie
- B. 1. to find gold
     2. to grow food
     3. to see the horses
     4. to stay warm
- C. 1. cleaned
     2. baked
     3. wanted

page 50:
- A. 1. b
     2. d
     3. f
     4. c
     5. a
     6. e
- B. 1. am reading
     2. eat
     3. is singing
     4. catches
     5. use
     6. are making

page 52:
- A. 1. How many
     2. How much
     3. How many
     4. How much
- B. 1. living things
     2. ecosystem
     3. earthworms
     4. tunnels
- C. 1. near
     2. on
     3. in the center of

page 60:
- A. 1. buffalo
     2. wigwam
     3. tepee
     4. pottery
     5. plains
     6. resources
     7. archaeologist
     8. insulator

- B. 1. circle "the Inuit"
     2. circle "the first Americans"
     3. circle "the Indians"

page 62:
- A. 1. circle "highlands"
     2. circle "statues"
     3. circle "pictographs"
     4. circle "foods"
- B. 1. before
     2. after
     3. When
     4. Then
- C. 1. made
     2. grew
     3. came
     4. had

page 70:
- A. 1. energy
     2. balanced diet
     3. fats
     4. carbohydrates
     5. proteins
     6. food pyramid
- B. 1. Yes, they did.
     2. No, he didn't.
     3. No, she didn't.

page 72:
- A. 1. chew
     2. stomach
     3. Digestion
     4. saliva
     5. Vitamins
- B. 1. across
     2. on
     3. next to
     4. in the distance

page 80:
- A. 1. e
     2. c
     3. a
     4. f
     5. b
     6. d
- B. 1. smaller
     2. longest
     3. harder
     4. noisier

page 82:
- A. 1. lumber
     2. crops
     3. minerals
     4. papayas
     5. rubber
     6. Spices
- B. 1. built
     2. cut down
     3. are working
     4. are harvesting

page 90:
- A. 1. north
     2. west
     3. region
     4. coast
     5. symbols
     6. capital

- B. 1. Each
     2. Some
     3. a lot of

page 92:
- A. 1. circle "long ago," "history," "last year"
     2. circle "today," "right now"
     3. circle "explorer"
     4. circle "time line"
     5. circle "visit places," "read books," "talk to people"
- B. 1. came
     2. built
     3. drove
     4. were

Listening Assessment

page 41: circle around western shirt, circle around cowboy boots, circle around cowboy hat; "x" on mountain, "x" on cattle, "x" on oil rig

page 43: top picture–2; second picture–4; third picture–1; bottom picture–3

page 51: top picture–3; second picture–1; third picture–4; fourth picture–2; fifth picture–6; bottom picture–5

page 53: Students' sentences should match tapescript on page T77 in the Teacher's Edition.

page 61: 1. circle tepee; 2. circle buffalo; 3. circle hammer; 4. circle clay pot

page 63: Students' sentences should match tapescript on page T115 in the Teacher's Guide;. top picture–3; second picture–4; third picture–1; bottom picture–2

page 71: circles around: milk, bananas, cereal, black beans, rice, apples, chicken, potatoes, oranges, ice cream

page 73: Students' sentences should match tapescript on page T153 in the Teacher's Edition.

page 81: Students should trace the path beside the two banana trees, the tree with the sloth, the stingray and snake, and the rubber tree.

page 83: top box–circle coconuts, pineapple, bananas, mangoes, papayas; middle box–circle cinnamon, cloves, nutmeg; bottom box–circle vegetable oil, nuts, coffee beans

page 91: Students' sentences should match tapescript on page T205 in the Teacher's Edition.

page 93: 1. circle 1822; 2. circle 1848; 3. circle 1850; 4. circle 1955; 5. circle 1984; 6. circle 1994